EXPERIENCE MINDFULNESS

How Quiet Time Makes You Feel

Jean C. Lawler

RED CHAIR
•PRESS•

Experience Personal Power books are produced and published by Red Chair Press

Red Chair Press LLC   PO Box 333   South Egremont, MA 01258-0333

www.redchairpress.com

FREE Lesson Plans from Lerner eSource and at www.redchairpress.com

Publisher's Cataloging-In-Publication Data

Names: Lawler, Jean C.

Title: Experience mindfulness : how quiet time makes you feel / Jean C. Lawler.

Other Titles: How quiet time makes you feel

Description: South Egremont, Massachusetts : Red Chair Press, [2018] | Series: Experience personal power | Interest age level: 007-010. | Includes bold words in context with a glossary and resources for further reading. | Includes index. | Summary: In this book children learn that being in the present moment and aware of what's going on right now helps them to be more focused, more patient, and more likely to make healthful decisions for themselves.

Identifiers: ISBN 978-1-63440-375-7 (library hardcover) | ISBN 978-1-63440-379-5 (paperback) | ISBN 978-1-63440-383-2 (ebook)

Subjects: LCSH: Mindfulness (Psychology)--Juvenile literature. | Emotions--Juvenile literature. | Self-control--Juvenile literature. | CYAC: Mindfulness (Psychology) | Emotions. | Self-controll.

Classification: LCC BF637.M56 L39 2018 (print) | LCC BF637.M56 (ebook) | DDC 158.12--dc23

LCCN: 2017948352

Illustrations by Nathan Jarvis

Photo credits: Coleman 17-20; Courtesy of the Author 24; iStock Cover, 1, 3-16, 22, 23

Printed in the United States of America

0518 1P CGBF18

Table of Contents

Getting Started:
Think About You

Which do you like to do most: read a book, listen to music, go for a walk outside?

How often do you feel peaceful?

What is your favorite thing to do when you are quiet?

Tune In to Mindfulness

What do you wonder about when you hear the word mindfulness? Perhaps being **aware** of what you are thinking? Maybe noticing your feelings? Possibly focusing on what's happening in your body?

Mindfulness is all three of these things. When you are mindful, you are aware of what you think, what you feel, and what's happening in your body.

It's about focusing on what's going on with you right now. It's about **tuning in to** yourself. You pay attention to your thoughts, your emotions, and your body. Mindfulness is a way to take care of yourself.

You can be mindful many times during your day. Take a minute to notice how you feel before you take a test. When you are asked a question, think about your answer before saying it. Before you go to sleep, wiggle each part of your body and then relax it. Anytime you want to quiet yourself down, you can be mindful.

Mindfulness can go everywhere with you. You can be mindful at your school desk, at home, or in the car by paying attention to your thoughts, your emotions, and how your body feels. You can be mindful while playing outside with friends. Or when you are inside by yourself watching TV or reading.

Take the time to slow down and notice how your thoughts and feelings can help you get to know yourself. Having a **balance** of busy time and quiet time is healthy for you. Being mindful helps you make choices that are right for you.

Your senses are handy mindfulness tools. Look out a window and focus on something you see, just for a moment. As you walk, pay attention to the sound your shoes are making. Enjoy the feel of a soft blanket around you. Take a deep breath in and notice if you detect any smells. At your next meal, notice which taste you like best of all.

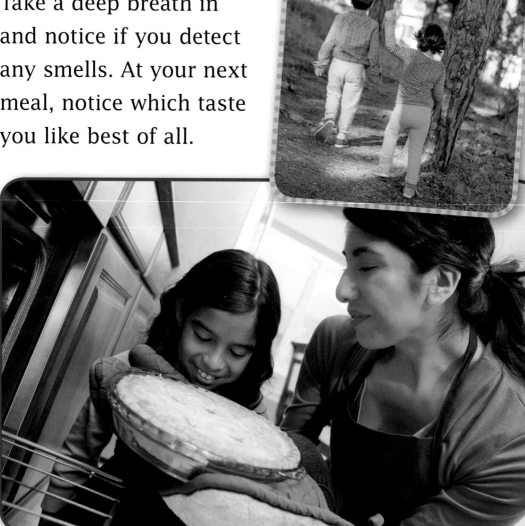

Sometimes it's hard to be mindful. There's a lot of noise around you. There's too much going on. Too many things to think about. It might be hard to make a choice. Your mind might feel like a monkey, jumping all around! Perhaps you feel worried or excited. Or you might get angry at someone for no reason. Your feelings are getting so strong! Mindfulness can help to give your body and brain a rest.

You can learn a lot about yourself by tuning in to mindfulness.

Make Sense of Mindfulness

There are so many ways that being mindful can help you feel good about yourself and find peace inside. It can make the difference between a good or bad day in school. It can make a difference in how well you get along with people. By practicing mindfulness, you can learn a lot about yourself and connect better to family and friends.

Start by being aware of what you are thinking and feeling inside your mind and body. Use your **inner voice** to connect to your thoughts. Sitting still with your eyes closed helps you pay attention to what you are thinking. Are you thinking about dinner? Your latest video game? Your science project? Name your thoughts.

Breathe in and out, slowly. Focus on your breathing. Notice your belly moving up and down. If your thoughts pop in, just return to your breath. What do you notice after a few deep breaths?

When you can calm your mind, your emotions, and your body, you have increased your personal power. When your mind is present, you can enjoy yourself and have fun with others.

You can make mindful choices for yourself. Mindfulness gives you the power to be a healthy, kind person.

Set a timer for 5 minutes. Close your eyes. Breathe in and out slowly. Listen to your own thoughts. What are you thinking and saying to yourself?

Check in with your emotions. How are you feeling?

Think about how your body feels, starting with your toes and working up to your head. Keep breathing until the timer rings. Notice how you feel after you open your eyes.

Start a journal page about times when you use mindfulness to calm yourself. Write down your thoughts, your feelings, or what was going on in your body. Write down what you did. Write down what changed when you were mindful.

The breathing exercises start with a "belly breath." Students breathe in through their noses and all the way down until their bellies rise. Then they breathe all the way out. This helps to clear their minds of thoughts that might keep them from having a good school day.

The Mindful Moment Room is a place where students can go when their feelings get too strong. They can practice deep breathing and talk about what's happening with them. They learn to get themselves back to a place of inner peace and calm.

Students place their hands on their bellies and breathe to calm their bodies and minds. They increase their personal power by learning when to do it and how to calm themselves. These kids are excited about sharing what they have learned with their parents and neighbors.

Moving On:
Taking Action Yourself

Plan some quiet time each day, like when you wake up and before you go to sleep.

Talk to your teacher about having Mindful Moments in your classroom, like just before a test, or after you come in from recess.

Ask your teacher if your class can set up a Mindful Moments Place in your classroom. Talk about what materials you would need to have a special quiet place there.

Share what you've learned about your inner voice and your personal power with your friends and family. Perhaps you can teach them about mindful choices.

Keep using your journal. Write and draw about how calming yourself makes you feel. Learning to know yourself helps build your personal power.

Index

About the Author

Jean Lawler is a busy teacher, wife, mother, and grandmother. She practices mindfulness every day. By finding a quiet spot and calming herself, she can hear her inner voice. It helps her be kind, happy, and grateful. Jean says that mindful choices make her life more *wonder*-ful!